ANIMALS IN OUR CARE
CATS

Written by
Rebecca Phillips-Bartlett

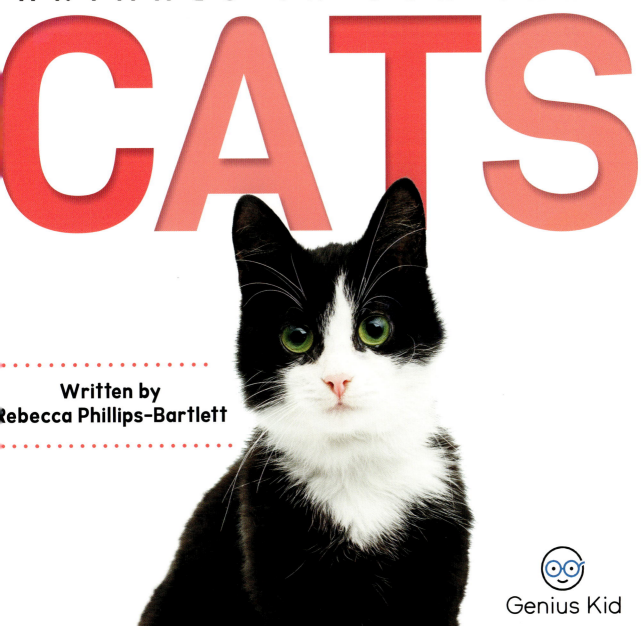

Genius Kid

American adaptation copyright © 2026 by North Star Editions, Mendota Heights, MN 55120. All rights reserved. No part of this book may be reproduced or utilized in any form or by any means without written permission from the publisher.

Cats © 2024 BookLife Publishing
This edition is published by arrangement with BookLife Publishing

sales@northstareditions.com | 888-417-0195

Library of Congress Control Number:
2024952951

ISBN
978-1-952455-35-3 (library bound)
978-1-952455-91-9 (paperback)
978-1-952455-71-1 (epub)
978-1-952455-55-1 (hosted ebook)

Printed in the United States of America
Mankato, MN
092025

Written by:
Rebecca Phillips-Bartlett

Edited by:
Elise Carraway

Designed by:
Ker Ker Lee

All facts, statistics, web addresses and URLs in this book were verified as valid and accurate at time of writing. No responsibility for any changes to external websites or references can be accepted by either the author or publisher.

Photo Credits – Images are courtesy of Shutterstock.com. With thanks to Getty Images, Thinkstock Photo and iStockphoto.

Cover – Anan Kaewkhammul, Andrey_Kuzmin, Eric Isselee, oksana2010, red-feniks, Tony Campbell, Vac1. 2–3 – ooodles. 4–5 – chrisbrignell, Eric Isselee, Jane Koshchina. 6–7 – jeep2499, Eric Isselee, Felineusl. 8–9 – KDdesign_photo_video, RJ22, Ukki Studio. 10–11 – Eric Isselee, Nynke van Holten, allme, Kirill Vorobyev. 12–13 – Nynke van Holten, Nejron Photo, Eric Isselee, 5 second Studio, Nynke van Holten, FCG, Evgeniia Trushkova, Irina Gutyryak. 14–15 – ANURAK PONGPATIMET, Dora Zett. 16–17 – Cat Box, Eric Isselee. 18–19 – Nataliia Maksymenko, Kuttelvaserova Stuchelova, Ermolaev Alexander. 20–21 – QBR, Max Acronym, BetterTomorrow, Vikafoto33. 22–23 – Max kegfirem, Andrey_Kuzmin, Eric Isselee, Vaclav Matous, Nynke van Holten.

CONTENTS

Page 4   Cats
Page 6   The Feline Family
Page 8   Feline Faces
Page 10   Body of a Cat
Page 12   Breeds and Colors
Page 14   Caring for Your Cat
Page 16   Body Language
Page 18   From Kitten to Cat
Page 20   Believe It or Not!
Page 22   Are You a Genius Kid?
Page 24   Glossary and Index

Words that look like <u>this</u> can be found in the glossary on page 24.

CATS

What do you think of when you hear the word *cat*?

Whether you think of cute kittens or roaring lions, these incredible creatures have a lot in common.

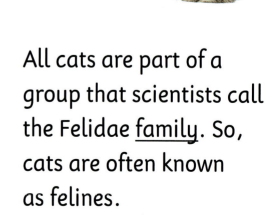

All cats are part of a group that scientists call the Felidae <u>family</u>. So, cats are often known as felines.

Cats are a type of mammal. They are warm-blooded and have a backbone. They make milk to feed their babies. Cats are also carnivores. They eat only meat.

Cats are known for being strong and graceful creatures.

THE FELINE FAMILY

Scientists have split the feline family into several smaller groups. These groups are based on how similar the cats are to each other.

The smallest known cat is the rusty-spotted cat. This wild cat weighs less than 4 pounds (1.8 kg).

Some small cats, such as <u>domestic</u> cats, are part of a group called *Felis*.

Many big cats are in a group called *Panthera*. This group includes lions and tigers. Most cats in this group can roar.

Cheetahs are in their own group. This group is called *Acinonyx*.

7

FELINE FACES

Let's look at the different parts that make up the face of a feline.

Cats have excellent eyesight, which helps them hunt their <u>prey</u>.

Cats use their whiskers to sense their surroundings.

Sharp teeth help cats rip meat apart.

Cats have 32 muscles in each ear. They move their ears around. They figure out where sounds are coming from.

Cats have rough tongues. Their tongues are covered in hook-like spines. These spines act as combs to help cats brush themselves. The spines also help wild cats lick bones clean.

BODY OF A CAT

Cats have flexible backbones. They can bend quickly and easily.

Long legs help cats leap and run quickly.

Claws in

Most cats have <u>retractable</u> claws. When cats do not need to use their claws, they keep them tucked away beneath their fur on their paws.

Strong muscles help cats climb.

Cats use their long tails to help them balance. They can also use their tails to show their feelings, such as if they're happy or afraid.

Claws out

DID YOU KNOW?
Cheetahs are the only cats that do not have retractable claws.

BREEDS AND COLORS

There are many different types of pet cats. These different types are called breeds. Unlike wild cats which have changed naturally over time, domestic breeds are controlled and changed by humans.

Persian cat

Sphynx cat

Ragdoll cat

Scottish fold cat

DID YOU KNOW?
There are at least 45 breeds of domestic cats.

12

Cats come in many different colors. They have <u>unique</u> patterns on their fur.

Tabby cat

DID YOU KNOW?
Most ginger cats are male.

Bicolor cat

Solid-colored cat

Tortoiseshell cat

Tortoiseshell cats have black and orange fur. Calico cats have black, orange, and white fur. Nearly all tortoiseshell and calico cats are female.

Calico cat

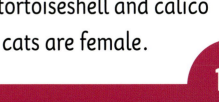
13

CARING FOR YOUR CAT

Pet cats have many of the same <u>instincts</u> as wild cats.

Cats are natural hunters. Stalking, pouncing, and playing with their prey keeps them happy. Cats enjoy playing in a way that lets them practice their hunting skills. Playing with your cat can also help you <u>bond</u> with each other.

DID YOU KNOW?
Stalking is when a cat slowly creeps toward something before pouncing.

Many things can scare cats. Cats should have their own space to hide, such as a cat tower. Do not disturb your cat while it is in its safe space.

Cats often feel safer up high. From there, they can see their surroundings.

A scratching post can help keep your cat's claws healthy.

BODY LANGUAGE

You can tell a lot about a cat's mood from what it does with its body. If a cat is <u>anxious</u> or worried, its eyes might be wide and round. Its ears will be flat. It might crouch down.

A scared cat might arch its back and puff out its fur.

A happy cat will have football-shaped eyes. It might hold its tail up high. A relaxed cat may roll on its back and show its belly.

DID YOU KNOW?
Cats purr for many different reasons. It does not always mean they are happy.

FROM KITTEN TO CAT

Cats go through different stages during their lives.

Baby cats are called kittens. Kittens are born with their eyes closed. Their eyes usually open when they are between one and two weeks old. Kittens drink milk from their mothers.

Kittens are very playful. When a kitten reaches one year old, it becomes an adult cat.

Adult cats may have kittens of their own. Domestic cats are <u>pregnant</u> for about 9 weeks. Most big cats are pregnant for about 15 weeks.

Cat

Kitten

BELIEVE IT OR NOT!

Cats were very important in ancient Egypt. Lots of ancient Egyptian gods looked like cats.

Most cats are most active early in the morning and late in the evening.

Bastet, an ancient Egyptian goddess

Just like a human fingerprint, every cat's nose print is unique.

Have you ever heard that cats almost always land on their feet? This happens because of the righting reflex. The righting reflex tells the cat which way is up. The cat's bendy backbone allows it to flip in the air and land on its feet.

ARE YOU A GENIUS KID?

Now you have plenty of incredible cat facts to wow your friends and family with. But first, it is time to test your memory and see whether you truly are a genius kid.

Check back through the book if you are not sure.

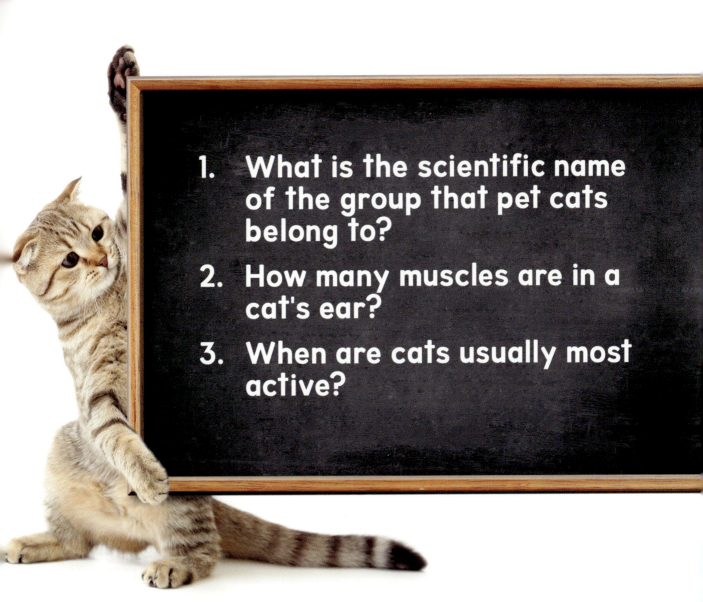

1. What is the scientific name of the group that pet cats belong to?

2. How many muscles are in a cat's ear?

3. When are cats usually most active?

Answers:
1. *Felis*, 2. 32, 3. Early in the morning and late in the evening.

GLOSSARY

anxious — worried or nervous
bond — to form a relationship based on love, friendship, and loyalty
domestic — when an animal is not wild and lives with humans
family — a group of animals with very similar traits
instincts — natural patterns of behaviors in animals
pregnant — when animals have babies growing inside them
prey — animals that are hunted by other animals for food
retractable — to pull back in
unique — one of a kind or very rare

INDEX

backbones 5, 10, 21
claws 10–11, 15
ears 9, 16, 23
evenings 20, 23
eyes 16–18
fur 10, 13, 17
kittens 4, 18–19
lions 4, 7
milk 5, 18
scientists 4, 6